TWENTY SENTRIES OF
BRISTLE
A.D. 50 – 1996

words by
DIRK ROBSON

pictures by
VIC WILTSHIRE & CHARLES WOOD

WESTCOUNTRY BOOKS

The original book *Sick Sundered Yers of Bristle*,
of which this is a revised and expanded version, was first
published in 1973 by Abson Books, Bristol.

Twenty Sentries of Bristle published in 1996 by Westcountry Books

British Library Cataloguing in Publication Data
CIP Catalogue Record for this book is available from the British Library

ISBN 1 898386 27 7

WESTCOUNTRY BOOKS
Halsgrove House
Lower Moor Way
Tiverton EX16 6SS
T: 01884 243242
F: 01884 243325

Printed by Culm Print Ltd., Tiverton

INTRODUCTION

This is much more than a book. Soaked in water, and then manipulated with the fingers, it will give hours of harmless fun. A man in Norfolk bought two copies and made a model of Vera Lynn singing 'We'll Meet Again' (b/w 'White Cliffs of Dover'). The chairman of the East Anglian Arts Council, Lord Cardboard, went out of his way to praise the rugged natural texture of the recycled material, and it was a pity that he went so far out of his way (West Kilbride) that his remarks were not more widely reported.

An interesting footnote is that the Norfolk artist promised to eat not only his words but ours too, if his work was not accepted by the Royal Academy; and we should all bear in mind the coroner's remarks that no blame attaches to the publishers in any way. "This is, or was, a book of the finest quality," he said, "a book that any frustrated and demented artist of no ability should be proud to eat, provided he remembered to leave the staples on the side of his plate." The verdict of death by rank stupidity was warmly applauded by the deceased's widow.

What more is there to say? A dozen copies of this splendid book will hold down that corner of the kitchen lino which keeps curling up; and two dozen copies will line the bottom of a parrot's cage for three years (or three parrots' cages for one year), provided you stick to a diet of organic nuts. The parrot can eat what it likes, of course.

Larson E. Whipsnade

LARSON E. WHIPSNADE
Bulk petfood, divorce enquiries & blocked drains (24 hours)

A.D.50
The Romans come looking for Bristle, slightly too early

Glevum was Gloucester, and Aquae Sulis was Bath. Roman roads led from them to Sea Mills, where the harbour was handy for South Wales. The Romans completely bypassed Bristle, mainly because it wasn't there. Incidentally, Annum was named after the Viking explorer, Per Annum.

The Dark Ages
Bristle folk get fed up with wading the Avon

Some time between the Romans and the Normans, the locals built a bridge from the bog that was to be Bedminster to the marsh that became Broadmead. They called the place Brig Stowe, or 'Bridge Place'. Later they stuck an L on the end to keep the dust out.

1171
Henry II gives Bristle the right to inhabit Dublin

A lot of Bristle folk went and lived in Dublin, and a lot of Irishmen knocked large lumps out of them. This behaviour was considered Beyond The Pale, but the Irish kept it up.

1373

Bristle gets a charter from Edward III

This turned the city into a county. When asked why, the king said it would keep Sumorsaetesshire apart from Glowcessestersshire; and it might give Wyllettesshire summit to think about, too.

1497

Cabot sails from Bristle for America!

The sturdy west-country name of John Cabot actually concealed the true identity of Giovanni Caboto, an Italian from Genoa, who had come to Bristle to find a boat. Look it up if you don't believe me.

1574

Queen Elizabeth I visits Bristle

The queen is said to have given Bristle women the freedom to dry clothes on Brandon Hill, since they were so ugly they'd never get married without this privilege. She was probably jealous. (Who did *she* marry, anyway?)

1634
First known reference to Bristle Milk sherry

There was much trade between Bristle and Spain. They gave us gert big barrels of Bristle Milk. We gave them jellied elvers and Cheddar cheese. On balance, we did better than they did.

1640

Bristle was England's second biggest port – provided the tide was in

Large sailing ships came up the Avon, but sometimes the Avon went out before they reached the port of Bristle. At low tide the river was a ditch. Nothing to do but sit and wait.

1642

Colonel Washington's fire-pikes break the siege of Bristle

This siege was settling down nicely and looked like having a long run, when Washington cheated by attacking a weak spot in the defences. His men tied blazing straw to their pikes, too. Shocking bad form.

1685
Judge Jeffreys threatens to hang Bristle's mayor for kidnapping

The mayor was guilty, but Jeffreys was bottled (as usual), so in the end he just fined him £1,000, which was a lot in those days. "I'll be glad when this Bloody Assize is over," the mayor said.

1739

John Wesley's open-air preaching to Kingswood miners scandalises the Bristle gentry

Wesley's bosses in the C of E reckoned that open-air services were indecent; but there weren't any churches in Kingswood, and in any case Wesley's congregations ran to thousands.

1780

Hotwells Spa – full of the quick and the dead

Hotwells water did nobody much good, and the visiting invalids keeled over at a rate of knots. The hotelkeepers doubled as undertakers, so they made their money one way or another.

1804

Digging the New Cut to divert the Avon past the Floating Harbour

The estimated cost of the Cut was £200,000, but they hit problems – like solid rock – and it took £580,000 and five years before the 2-mile channel was dug.

1807

Parliament votes to abolish Bristle's pot of gold, the slave trade

The Merchant Venturers kicked and screamed and said it spelled doom for Bristle – but they soon shut up, because most of the slave trade had already gone to Liverpool, anyway.

1831

Queen Square sacked and Mansion House looted in Bristle Riots

The trouble started over Parliamentary reform, but when the mob broke into the Corporation's wine-cellars under the Mansion House, politics took second place. The politicians vanished pretty fast, too.

1843

The launching of the S.S. 'Great Britain'

A great day for Bristle, or was it? The *Great Britain* was the biggest ship afloat – too big to get back up the Avon, so she had to use Liverpool. Hmm.

1848
The young W.G. Grace, Bristle's greatest cricketer, hits apples for six

W.G. was born in Downend. He and his five brothers (they all played for Gloucestershire) practised in the orchard, opening their shoulders to the Granny Smiths.

1940
Bristle in the blitz

Business went on as usual by day, but it got a bit noisy at night.

1973
Sick sundered yers on

Never mind what's happening up there; down here it's usually quicker to walk.

1996

After 23 years in the wilderness, Bristle triumphs again

In 1974, Avon robbed Bristle of the county status she'd had since 1373 – but not for long. Avon died, unlamented, in 1996. Bristle bounced back – both a city and a county again.

GLOSSARY

Aft Trawl	Taking everything into account
Annum	Suburb of Bristle
Ant Chew	Get on with it
Axe Dent	Small disaster
Bank Wits	Big meals
Barbara Stuffs	Roughnecks
Bart Nil	Area of Bristle between Reckliff and Lorne's lll
Bit Rail	Basic beer
Bren Jam	Basic grub
Bleed Nell!	Goodness Gracious!
Brassy Air	Feminine uplift
Connive	Gimme
Counts Louse	Bristle's centre of government
Crates	Produces; manufactures
Deaf Knit Lea	Certainly; without doubt
Deck Rated	Given a medal
Diesel Lava	You'll get a
Fairy Nuff	Suits me
Fey Sit	Admit the facts
Fig Red	Statue at sharp end of ship
Forgots Ache	Expression of strong feeling
For Peace Ache	Heartfelt appeal
Furze	As far as
Grace Tepp-Ford	Big progress
Grape Leisure	Much enjoyment
Grape Written	Antique steamship
Grey Skids	W.G.'s offspring
Guess Tuck Interim	Give them what-for
Haddock Rate Big	Used to be a lot larger
Ham Rum	Give 'em hell
Ice Pecked	It seems likely
Jeer	Let me draw your attention to
Juice Pose	What's your opinion?
Juicy That?	Or do my eyes deceive me?
Krek Waiter	Textbook method
Libel	Likely or inclined
Mike Cod	Good heavens!
Mines	Brains

Moira Wave-Life	Not so much a job
Money Art Noon	Early in the week
Numb Rate	Between 7 and 9
Nutters Candle	An absolute disgrace
Office Ed	Daft
Pain Noah Tension	Ignore it
Perry Shin	Infuriating; blasted
Poor Twine	Stimulating after-dinner beverage
Port Zed	Coastal town near Bristle
Posse Bull	Can be done
Puss Sup	Raises; increases
Quince Dense	Simultaneous happenings
Race	Local taxes
Rice Choir	I agree with you, sir
Saul Finched	The end
Saviour Breff	Don't excite yourself
Scar	A damn good smoke
Serge Asper	Notorious baronet
Sink Ready Bull	I don't believe it
Smite Urn	I'm next
Snuff	That'll do
Sorry Fine	Most disturbing
Stans Treason	Commonsense indicates
Star Craven	Barking
Stray Ted	Follow your nose
Swarm; Sot	Up the thermometer; further up
Thin Tweet	Food
Throne	Chucked
Tomb Erica	Across the Atlantic
Tour Free	Less than 4
Trite Homer Bout	To boast of
Twang	To suspend
Usure Red	Think about it
Why-Cello	A pale shade
Wine Tea	He's got a better option
Wop Rices	How much is
Wreck Non	Depend on
Yuma Fool, Incher?	Another fine mess you got me into